the pause and the breath

KWAME SOUND DANIELS

atmosphere press

praise for
the pause and the breath

"As I read Kwame Daniels' collection, I was reminded of Keats' definition of poetry as 'the vale of soul-making.' Daniels' project of soul-making—of finding authentic selfhood—is urgent and ambitious. It involves a reckoning with trauma, illness, racial injustice, and systemic homophobia. It *also* involves a radical re-envisioning of that most venerable of poetic forms, the sonnet, and for Daniels the sonnet is both a talisman against iniquity and a vehicle for hard-won celebration. As xe write in a poem entitled 'ars poetica - ars trans - black poetica,' 'It exists in space—the pause and the breath. / It is the almost-thought, the precipice / from which feet dangle. Hands hover. Fingers / press. Words tumble out.' Kwame Daniels is a poet of unusual promise."

- David Wojahn, author of *World Tree*

"'I is another' wrote Rimbaud. 'The me-that-was-not-me was warped and my / reflections never quite reflected what / was real. I didn't know what was real,' writes Kwame Daniels in 'The Mirror.' In this amazing book of unrhymed sonnets Daniels explores the complexities of selfhood through a mirror, yes, but also through a lens that includes 'dead women at the foot of my bed,' lost mothers, friends and grandmothers, for it is the 'cold press of their breath [that] weighs on my heart.' In this way xe can, on the one hand, define xemself as 'the absence / of absence,' but also, as xe say in 'ars poetica – ars trans – black poetica,' as a self that 'exists in space—the pause and the breath.' Which is to say the superb breath, the original voice and vision that constitutes *the pause and the breath*. Indeed, this is a book that will steal your breath as it did mine, and open the door to the self's endless possibilities."

- Richard Jackson, author of
The Heart as Framed: New and Select Poems

"Perception is not an act of understanding."

—Maurice Merleau-Ponty, Phenomenology of Perception

Morning

You weigh yourself. Put on your jacket. You
walk your dog. Drag her away from roadkill.
Pick up her shit. Put on a dress. Drive to
the grocery store. Get a few donuts. Eat
them. Wait for the cramping. Take a shit. Weigh
yourself again. Think about how much less
you will weigh without your breasts. Think about
your decision to grow your hair out and
how it feminizes you. Decide that
you can't afford to care. Your hair journey
is too important. Loving your routines
is too important. Caring for yourself
is too important. Don't think about work.
Just write. Just breathe. The day has just begun.

Ungendered 1

Three dead women at the foot of my bed.
They watch. They murmur. But I don't speak this
language, the language of binding the bound.
What can I offer them but my mind? Tears
drip from brown eyes. Hair loc'd and beaded. I
think of my own black curls. I have two white
hairs for each of them because I have no
tears. I am witness. I am scribe. And yet—
I wonder when that will be me, standing
at the foot of someone's bed in a white
nightdress. Will someone cry for me? Will they
speak my language? Words from an ungendered
spirit: I barely know how to speak them.
When will I be fluent in my own tongue?

COCSA

I WAS NEVER A GIRL—THAT WAS STOLEN
NEVER-BEEN-TOUCHED UNTIL I WAS AND THEN
I HAD TO LEARN WHAT UNGIRLHOOD WAS HAD
TO BE MADE AND UNMADE HAD TO STEAL IT
BACK FROM HER WITHOUT KNOWING WHAT THEFT
  WAS
IT WAS BLACK ON BLACK ON BLACK CRIME IT WAS
A FATHER REACHING THROUGH HIS DAUGHTER TO
DO HARM IT WAS A MAN TOUCHING WITHOUT
SEEING THE LIFE HE INVADED—WORMING
AND SQUIRMING HANDS THE UN-GIRLING OF A
NOT-QUITE-A-GIRL-NOT-YET HE STOPPED IT ALL
HE SPOKE THROUGH HIS DAUGHTER'S MOUTH
   WITH A VOICE
THAT SHOOK THE HEAVENS WITH THE QUIET WHEN
MY SKY CRACKED MY SHELL RE-SHAPED I VANISHED

On Motherhood

Unblossomed seed, I wanted to birth you.
I wanted to hold you in my arms, day-
dream about how I might be called *mother*
in another life. Yes, another you,
another me. Oh, so delicate you
are, flower-that-never-was. With your small
brown hands grasping mine. Our eyes would meet. My
heart would pause. Oh and I'm proud of what I
would have done. I would have strained for hours to
bring you into this world. The soft wisps of
hair, dark as peat, feathery as mine were
when I was born, the beginnings of a small
dimple in your plump cheek. Little one,
stay close to me. All my life, I'll love you.

My dead

I don't know them. They hover around me
and whisper, touch my shoulders, but I don't
know them. Tired, I sit and let them chatter.
I cannot speak. The silence is for them.
They fill the space in the room, wispy and
translucent. They tell me grief will pass, hurt
will dull, and the knife of urgency will
no longer cut me. I wish I knew their
names. I want to open my mouth, whisper,
but I know I can't. They need more time
to speak to each other, to lay to rest
their obsessions, to work through their wisdom.
The cold press of their breath weighs on my heart
and I wait, palms open, and I listen.

MIRROR

1

The me-that-was-not-me was warped and my
reflections never quite reflected what
was real. I didn't know what was real.
The mirror has lied to me since childhood.
Smiles that curled too wide, eyes bulbous and red,
hair a tangle, teeth sharp points. What was I?
My mother called me *whore, demon.*
Age eight: *jezebel.* I didn't know what
a whore was, but I knew that's what I was
becoming. Commodifying my form
for sex-hunger and love, trying to look
appealing as a child. Black girls transformed
into women by the gaze of sick men.
Nice Legs, an old man told me. I was ten.

2

There is a reflection of a not-me
in the mirror. There is a cool breeze that
lifts their hair. Wild eyes and a curling smile—
rows of shark teeth, a black tongue. This is who
I see. This is why I avoid mirrors
everywhere. Hands that curl
into fists, fingers that wiggle and reach—
this isn't something that I wanted to
see. When my mother called me *Monster*, I
began to see this thing. I can't hear it
but I hear its shrieks. I see mania
shimmering like an aura. Fat body,
rake-thin. My Eidolon with wild hair and
slits for eyes, I wish I never knew you.

3

Constantly digging the dirt from under
my nails. Washing, always washing,
trying to scrub away the feeling of
skin. Can't look at myself, can't look at the
thickness of my fingers or the padding
of my palms. Let my blackness stay. Let it
be more than a strange phrenological
mythos and summer color. What is the
shape of being black? What lies beyond the
caricature? Cleanliness is freedom.
It is the unburdened march toward joy.
It is the bar of soap for the enslaved.
This is what my ancestors had wished for.

4

I wish that cowrie shells looked good on me.
I wish I could braid them into locs that
run past my shoulders but when I look at
myself, I see a figure ill-suited
to the remains of an ocean-dweller.
I see two curl patterns—one from my birth
mother, one from my birth father. I see
red undertones in my brown skin. I see
a small nose. Is it enough? Am I? When
is the legacy of the mother not
a condition of the child? When am I
permitted a winter tone? Dates have looked
me over, trying to find my real skin,
as if the one I'm wearing doesn't count.

5

My belly jiggles. I don't like to look
at it in the mirror; it expands when
I breathe or folds when I bend, sagging a
little from weight loss. Stripes of scar tissue
that used to itch when they were new and raw
band the skin. My skin itches now. Dryness
came with the cold. White stripes marking the trail
of my fingernails. Little flakes on my
hip. My belly is never dry, always
soft. Are animals ever this fat? Are
they ever this soft? Cramping and throbbing
pains. Needles in my gut. Nails pinning me
on a corkboard wall. Glass case surrounding
me. Mirror, please, don't look at my belly.

6

My cane makes me look like a mermaid. It
has a teal scale pattern and glow-in-the-
dark nubs. It rests against the wall in my
room, but I don't use it. Not really. In
the story, whenever she walks on land,
the little mermaid is in pain. Let me
write this mythopoeic fiction. I get
that. Water takes the stress of gravity
off my tendons; I swim easily. But
I only get to look like a mermaid
on land, when I'm too hurt to hold myself
upright without assistance. So then, where
is the freedom in movement? My spine is
tired. Let me rest. Let me breathe. Let me think.

Birth mother

Could my mother weave? Did she know the stars
by heart? Could she sing their brightness? I think
that she had lakes for eyes, imagine them
brown as the dirt at the bottom where
axolotls would swim, eyes so big they
could swallow the moon. Her
hair grows out of the top of my head, jet
black curls that catch the sunlight and hold it.
I want to learn my family's wisdom,
want to say, "Teach me Maya womanhood
for I know nothing of the shape of it."
I want to know my ancestor's pronouns.
How did language form matrilineal
bonds? Where can I find my birth mother's love?

Cookfire

Where was my grandmother? In a cookfire.
In the ashcake.
            Where was my grandfather?
In the ache of bones. In my eyes.
                  Where was
my father? In the width of my smile. In
my rage.

      Where was my sister? In a glance.
In trepidation.
           Where was my brother?
In capital. In story.

          My cousin?
In a meeting place. In shrewd looks.

And my ancestor? In the grip of my
hands. In the fat of my arms.

                  Where was my
friend? In a kiss. In our hands touching.

Where was my mother? In the stirring of
soup. In the steaming of a tamale.

Where was I? In dancing ghosts on paper.

The Body

I take the skeleton of my want and
dance. We swirl and twirl, mixing flesh and death,
white on life, absence and breath. Brown skin, brown
skin. The ancestor clacks their jaw at me.
"I can't hear you," I say, "can't understand."
We stop dancing. We sit. "What do you make
of this?" I pinch my fat. My ancestor
rattles. I look at my stomach. A hand
touches it. "I wish I knew what you were
saying," I murmur. I'm hungry in a
way my ancestor never knew. I
clack my own jaw, try to stretch the tendon.
Empty eye sockets stare into me. I
close my eyes. There is much that I don't know.

Pronouns

I am not a they. I am the absence
of absence. I am the whippoorwill cry.
I am school cafeteria pizza.
I am an unstable decoction. I
am ice in a mug. I am cooling tea.
I am the steam from a kettle. I am
sorrel. I am chiffonade basil. I
am a mother sauce. I am cloves speared in
an onion. I am simmering heavy
cream. I am the clang of weights on a floor.
I am a julienned carrot. I am
the mint in lentil soup. I am dog hair
on a blanket. I am rosemary in
a botanical garden. I am xe.

I'm trans like

a frog on a lilypad, waiting for
the breath to submerge, resting in dappled
sunlight, evening sky rosy with the
ebb of day, feeling moonlight tugging
at my heart, my cool body small and green,
letting the water hold me in gentle
ripples, my tongue retracted, cheeks empty,
eyes blinking away the breeze, webbed toes spread
wide for balance, legs bent in readiness,
haunches bunched, muscles coiled,
toes bunched, underbelly pale yellow,
the yellow of a kindness done to hands
trembling with fatigue, the color of care,
gentle mouth closed with whispers of light.

Surgery

The soul runs adjacent to the body.
In the roots of the forest lies all that was built,
trees that stand still, ageless and aging, rings
that hold the truth. And here is the truth: time
is fractured. The selves split. Some parts of
the forest grow faster than others. Some
parts are nourished. Life perseveres and the
body keeps going. Humans are
mutable. Just ask the stars. Their silence
is another language. At night, when all
of the forest is quiet—that is when
they speak. The speech is in the shine, leaves that
rustle and breach. Here's the truth: time is told
in tears. And the count of days lies in rest.

Movement

Like each petal on a chrysanthemum
we are movement. We are flash yellow and
soft sweetness. We pair well with honey. We
are auspicious. We are for kings. And each
flower holds potential. Every garden
grows with healing. That's what everyone says,
anyhow. I want someone to drink my
entanglement the way we drink ourselves.
Companionship swells with each gulp. What is
a partner to a queer like me? Someone
who is distant from the body, who will
hesitate to embrace another? What
does touch mean for a petal easily
torn? My body must reconcile with me.

Absence

the word asẹ is like energy or
spirit. It is that which lives, beyond life.
And where does the spirit reside in me?
In this? Womanhood doesn't touch
me here. There is a chasm within my
waters deep. Unfathomable. And I
can't explore it. It was not meant to be known.
My making gifted this part of me. That
is part of the whole. This absence
grants me life, grants me the   leap   into dark
drag of expression—the night inherent
in performance. The night is ours. The night
is trans. The sun sets on gender. I
glow. This is asẹ. This is my spirit.

Dance

I sway my hips as my mothers
would, I hear the call of the spirits as feet
stomp. Ripples in my flesh like water as
I whine and twist. Spit rum into open
flame. Wind dances across my skin. Linen
white dress flares as I spin. I shout as I
circle in the ring. I welcome spirits
in. They ride my body as I do, there
and not-there, above and within. Secret
places are made in my soul. It is night.
The heat of the day keeps the ground warm. Dirt
under my feet keeps me humble. The rum
on my tongue lets me welcome the spirits.

Hunger

I taught myself I had to be hungry
for my own gender, that I had to carve
out a bowl to hold androgyny
that I could never achieve being fat.
I painted myself with emphatic oils,
I fired myself in my own fear. Not once
did I crack under the heat. My hunger
was well-made, developed. There was no
filling me. I became content with what
I knew. I kept myself starved because it
was safer than knowing. My truth was in
the absence. Falsehoods were the feminine,
until the feminine satisfied the
appetite I cultivated for love.

Rumi

Wait for the cut and the recovery.
The heart resides in the hands. How shall I
live? How shall I keep my head held high, my
mouth pursed, anticipating? This is how
the heart touches the world. This is how hearts
of doctors touch me. They shape my body
the way I dreamed it. That is the future.
This is the past; every moment that is
lived has been. Chickpeas have already been
soaked and boiled. Collards have already been
sauteed. Season with salt and harissa.
Allow grace before the event. Soften
your gaze. Forgiveness takes rest. And now
the world will hold its breath for your body.

3b 3c

I was afraid of what it might mean to
have corkscrew curls sprouting from my head, to
have petals of lazy ringlets frame
my face. Something ethereal about
the way they hang—ivy on a trellis
leaning toward sunlight. A waxy gleam
bringing a soft glow to the deep-soil black.
Daffodil soft and springing, uncontained.
I had to learn how to bow in the face
of feminization; I came to love
the way my curls held water. It's enough
that I leave the scent of roses on my
pillow, that I anoint my scalp with oil
so shoots of lavender grow from my crown.

TIME

1

Days spent prone in bed, bolstered by pillows,
wishing my dog would move because she is
setting my hip on fire with her body
but knowing she won't. Walks take twice as long
during weeks with rain. Legs don't move right. Each
step feels like a stretch, jerky—uneven
over grass. Time around me slows while hours
rush by. Night is my time. Night is winding
down. Night is a body suspended. But
the nights of my friends go differently. I
live in a time adjacent to others.
I watch through my phone screen as they dance and
walk and gather. I yearn. Wishing that time
would move at my pace, that the world would slow.

2

Am I mad to exist, to wear a dress,
to go outside knowing my body will
be devoured by the eyes of others? The
petulant, feminine anger I have
cultivated—not the physical rage
from before the realization of trans
identity—is simmering. Brown skin,
black cascade. Am I mad when I feel bugs
crawling in my ears? Am I mad when I
am convinced they will eat my brain? Total
loss of feeling in my left leg. I try
to walk fast when a man is behind me,
as if he couldn't catch me. He is made
monster through fear and loathing.

3

Intransitive being, you wished for one
more chance at childhood, wished for your body
to be remade. You look to the future,
taking each day as the already-past.
When the scalpel cuts your breasts you'll become
again and each dream you have will be stitched
in where your breasts were. There's hope in your chest
and fear on your tongue, but you keep dreaming.
You are living each moment suspended.
The years before don't count. You swore
to yourself the weight of your breasts wouldn't
make your soul heavy. So you close your eyes
and pray to the ancestors for healing,
and you wait for the day when you'll be new.

4

I hadn't felt the touch of a woman's
lips until I was twenty-five. Hadn't
known that it would feel like coming home. Soft
and sweet-smelling. Bumping noses until
we found each other again. I learned
what I wanted when I was fourteen but
I was afraid. There were so many things
I thought I would get wrong. There is no right
age to know woman-love, I understand
that now. Maybe my queerness was sleeping.
Maybe it needed to be tended,
so that it might thrive; the soil wasn't right.
But I'm here now, still worried about how
late I am, scared to let my new growth show.

5

You sit there clenching and unclenching your
fists, waiting for the rolling waves of bugs
under your skin to pass, waiting for hot
weights on your chest to cool. You wish for a
shower but you can't take one. Too afraid
of nakedness. You shudder. You don't know
when this will pass. Sometimes it stretches through
the whole day. Your head jerks. You can feel them
in your ear now, making their way to your
brain, eating you alive. You try not to
think about the way your breasts jiggle when
you slap your ear to dislodge the bugs. You
want to pray but you only believe in
insects that sit in your skin like diamonds.

6

Close my eyes. Open them. It's dark. Close my
eyes. Open them. Bright points flaring in my
hips, blinding heat, knives edging the bones apart.
It's light. Beams through my window. Branches
waving gently in the wind. The sun won't
move. Hangs overhead with a pressing eye,
gazing upon me, still and weak. I wish
I could raise my arms. But I'm so tired. I
try to flex my fingers, but the joints ache.
My hand is swollen, glovelike. My toes are
the only things that don't hurt, but I can't
wiggle them. So I close my eyes. Open
them. I wish it could be the day's beginning.
The sky is orange. I wish it were pink.

7

reverie of a noose tightening around
your neck, lungs burning, tongue laying thick and
heavy out of your mouth and of water
choking you—getting lost in an endless
blue and knowing peace after a struggle,
a lifetime of pains inflicted by white
family who don't know any better
because their reality is different
from yours—you, mad, crazy, reality
bent and warping, ceilings move and heave and
the ground swirls and shadow people stand
at the edge of your vision walking to
you but never touching, never clear—is
this what your ancestors would have wanted?

Body

I've spent all day curled up in bed, trying
not to let my breasts touch my arms, trying
not to be aware of the bra strap (it
digs into my shoulder), holding my piss
so I don't have to endure the touch of
wiping my vagina when I'm done. I
shut my eyes. I open them. My brain is
on fire and my thoughts careen about with
a dread that I haven't felt in a long
time. This is not what I was meant to be—
clenching my teeth so hard my jaw hurts
and trying not to feel my own skin. When
I was a child, I had wanted better
for myself than a body, unable.

architect

I will become the architect of my
own body. How many bodies will I
go through before I'm done? And how many
iterations of self are there? What can
I do with a body like mine, recent
colonoscopy notwithstanding. I
can't look at myself. I can't stand my own
face, the way it glowers. How do I construct
what I cannot see? How do I move the
fat and build muscle or make organs work
the way I need them to? This isn't fair.
My illness won't let me. Shun the body.
Pain from pain. Fatigue from pain. Every
joint is crackling with the weight of the day.

Breastmilk

A stain. Wet shirt-front. Cold. Connection to
the self. The subjective, conceptual.
Find me. Womanmystic. Ungendered. Not-
person, notwoman. Never once a girl.
How came this to be? White, flecked with gold. I
produce gold. I make knowledge. Value me.
If there ever was a baby to pour
myself into it would be healthy. It
would glow. Visions of the dark mother cloud
my eyes. If only I could be the one.
Unthinking child. How could you? Grown into
that which forsakes knowing, that which I gifted.
I don't let myself dream. If you could call
it that. I think myself the exception.

Couldn't leave

You were heartbroken. You left the kettle
on the stove too long, let the steam scream in
a burst from the lid. Your legs were pins and
needles and your jaw was clenched. You tried to
blink away the burning in your eyes. But
the tears came. Your chest echoed with pain. You
could hear sobs. Didn't realize they were yours.
Your body was the one thing you couldn't
leave. Wanting to tear the fat from your skin,
wanting to cut off your breasts with your chef's
knife. Saw at the flesh until it was done,
thought about your hips, digging your fingers
into them until they throbbed. Just try to
drink your oolong before it gets cold.

soared

Last night I dreamed I soared through the ocean
with infant humpback whales. In each hand one
of their fins as we flipped and swooped in the
blue expanse. The waters were clear. They went
all the way down. There was no need for air;
my lungs were full with joy. I could only
hum my pleasure. I could only hope that
they heard me. In that body, there was no
weight and I had no breasts, the better to
glide through the water. The sea was quiet
as bridges collapsed and the land fell to
the water but I was safe and agile
and soft. Scars on my chest were dark. Down deep,
I hadn't known the meaning of *transgender*.

Chorus

Piety lies in the moon. Promises
you make to her, whispered in the dark when
she shines her face on you. Don't hide. Bring trust
closer to your heart. Retain nourishment.
Remember you must learn. The humming starts.
A rise and fall of the chest. A prophet
begins to sing in a low rasp. And a
harmony swells. Many voices lift high.
The chorus is in you. The body will
change by the touch of many hands. Playful,
not like a baby animal. No, like
the hair that floats to the floor from my head.
Community lies in the ring. Vows coast
on the shout. And you know the way to step.

Two-spirit

Black American rootworker, I pray
to the ancestors, ask the spirits for
guidance. I make tinctures and glycerites
and bath teas. I wonder at my me-ness,
the culmination of two bloodlines of
shamans, disjointed delineated
knowledge learned secondhand, healing borne of
meditation. Two-spirit, the twining
of metaphysics and embodiment,
askance in a voice, a shout hurled into
the air—Ancestors, weave me a dress.
Step out of the grave to dance my dance.
Linger on in my presence. Tell my story
in the pattern, bear my heart in the colors.

Mami Wata

Count my worth in cowrie shells from the sea,
pluck all my visible scales. Let me swim
in my waters, let my hair grow long and
thick, let it be as a black cloud under
water. Let the fins between my fingers
remain uncut and filmy. Do not send
me back if I've forgotten how to breathe.
May I honor the graves of the dead in
the Atlantic; sit on the ocean floor
and be. Let my heart be still, let me float
into the dark, let me feel the comfort
of pressure on my skin. Put me back in
the water so that I may once again
taste the salt of the open blue and sing.

Nesting

I want my scars to be touched tenderly.
I want the future lines on my body
to be loved, the marks on my belly to
be stroked. But I am so afraid that it
won't happen, that I won't get to see my
partner's slow sly smile, that I won't get to
hold hands in the grass under the sun. I'm
afraid that once I get surgery, I
won't be beautiful anymore. Who taught
me to leave breasts untouched? Who taught me that
altering the body was a sin? This
will be a sin that comes with healing and
the joy of looking at oneself in the
mirror. I'll get closer to becoming.

Church

My mother dressed me in tulle, painted my
face with a blush that didn't show well. White
frills on brown skin, congruous but forced. She
kept me in a corner, had me clad in
dresses and skirts that she made herself with
material from Walmart. Pantyhose
tight and irritating, slipping with each
step. Shiny black shoes scuffed from play on deep
red carpet. Church smelled like bread and wine. She
bid me stay quiet, stop giggling, permed
curling hair bobbing. So I didn't laugh.
I stood with my hands clasped over my skirt,
itching from lace, and staring at the cross
on which Christ died, gauging the weight of sin.

Weights

I think, maybe if my breasts were smaller,
then I would keep them. The fierce disdain
for my body wouldn't be so acute—
maybe I'd handle the bounce if the bounce
were less emphatic—I wouldn't abhor
the way they hang and swing when I lean or
when they just flop to the side when I lay
down. Useless. I keep thinking if this weren't
so, then I wouldn't need surgery, like
I could achieve perfect androgyny
if my breasts were barely there, a modest
A cup, concealable and quiet. Not
these attention-stirring weights that have been
grabbed and handled and punched and slapped by men.

Leak

It's cloudy. Didn't you know? Couldn't you
see my wet shirt? Couldn't you see my face?
I embarrass myself over this. Not
in public. Only at home, where it's safe.
Force an earring through the hole in my lobe.
It's been so long. Bleeding. Crusty. It's all
closed. Everything. The gold hoop hangs heavy.
Take comfort in the weight, in the curve of
bright metal. I can be bright too. But wait
for me. Just give me a chance to get it
right. I'm out of practice. I hadn't worn
a dress in years. I rejected the soft
material. Dressed in my ex's clothes.
Now I have to unclench my jaw to speak.

To myself

You were the invention of door-slamming,
the taut mixture of the binding feminine,
the ache of re-discovery. I
discovered you. Uncovered you. Hiding,
small, like paws tucked under a belly, like
retractable claws. Sitting there with your
hands over your eyes. You don't see yourself,
how you look to me. You salt yourself to
taste. Paprika on patatas bravas.
Savory. A little parsley like it's
the eighties. Out-of-mode for the time. Still
weaving those tales of fear. Trifling. And still
making the masculine your blankie. Well,
no one taught you better than that, did they?

Snake venom

It's arresting—biting, the way it sears
the veins—cauterizes seeping hatred.
End-stopped cries muffled and barred.

She.

It used

to make me nauseous to be gendered as
a woman, used to make my muscles scream
and tighten, used to make my heart drop down
to my belly. I paced. Took shuddering
breaths. Chest too constricted to breathe steady.
Air tasted stale. Fingertips tingled. Teeth
ached. Face heated. The pronoun settled on
me as would a shirt of thorns. But I learned
not to fixate on gendering from the
outside. A wound many-times spoken, a
simple little word, thoughtlessly uttered.

can't

I shower for the first time in three days.
I've gone longer without. I feel stupid,
but still I let the water run over
me, run over my breasts. I take soap from
suave. not the best for my skin I know but
it makes me smell like violets and sweet
pea flowers, the scent inviting and soft.
I lather the soap in my loofah that
has a handle. I scrub. let the water
run. brush my hand over my vagina—
only the lightest of touches. it's all
I can bear. I don't look down. I don't
dare pay attention to the soft flesh.
soon, the water will make me clean again.

Recital

In childhood I thought woman-life was simple,
was wrapped in the gauze and tulle of tutus.
I thought my recitals displayed girlhood
as I leapt. I thought it was in my toes
en pointe or in a plié or the crook
of my arm as I raised it high. Act like
a lady, I was told, told to imbue
my steps with grace. I was always showing
off, proud of what I knew I would become,
though "lady" chafed and tore at me. My toes
were raw, sore. I felt like the stepsister
who cut off her heel to fit the glass shoe,
encouraged by her mother to do so.
Princesshood: a state I could not reach.

woman-hate

There were *broads* and there were *broads*. Looked in a
mirror—thought, *That's a pretty woman in
a dress.* Lost in the swish of a yellow
skirt. Soft fabric. High collar. Itched where the
tags were. Hem just above the knee. I looked
good. My masculinity was enmeshed
with woman-hate. But my woman-hate balked.
Made me sick. Couldn't look at my curves. Eyes
slid away from the edges of my ass
and hips. Iron-set jaw clenched. Gendering
was a horror. Womanhood was all rage.
Didn't want to be angry anymore.
So I swallowed my sickness and began
anew, taking triumph in my own will.

Ungendered 2

Not-woman, not-girl, not-man, I was not,
not, not anything that could be solid,
anything concrete, in stasis; I was
not a fan flicked open and fluttering,
not the swish of satin skirts, not a bow
at the nape of a neck, nor coquettish
batting of eyelashes; I couldn't be
the tweed of a jacket or patches at
the elbows, the smell of a tobacco plant,
the knife that cut the leaves from the stalk; I
wasn't white nylons, nor the run in them
caused by nails; I was neither sun nor moon;
I was not silken or lace lingerie.
I wear the fugitive space in blackness.

Mammy

You stand in the low lighting of a food
joint right by the soda machine. You are
wearing shorts and a zip-up hoodie. You
have just gotten out of class. You just want
two slices of new york style pizza. Cheese
and grandma style. You like this pizza joint.
The cooks are brusque and their eyes don't linger
on you as many men's eyes tend to. An
old woman appears at your side. She wears
a white cardigan over a yellow
shirt and blue pants. Her white hands give you her
cane and purse. You take them. You stand silent
while she got herself some sprite. She takes her
cane and purse and leaves you there, as you were.

Bodymind

The mind is in the spine, in the belly,
in the knees. It is in the hands curling
and uncurling, the way fingers straighten
out, muscles contracting, skin tightening.
Consciousness exists in bright blooms
of pain—an abrasion of knowing the
brain's physicality. All bundles of
nerves like many rivers flaring, rushing,
directing. The path of synapses ripple
with small bursts of lightning. The shift happens
pre-convergence. Touch sparks all knowing. The
sting is in the realization: you were
not two. You were one. So let yourself be
carried in these waters toward feeling.

ars poetica – ars trans – black poetica

It exists in space—the pause and the breath.
It is the almost-thought, the precipice
from which feet dangle. Hands hover. Fingers
press. Words tumble out. Nearly linear
impermanence. Shift states. Aqueous form.
Babypink antagonism. A true
wind blows North. Grass between the teeth. Vomit.
Spit. Expansive starbursts brighten the sky.
An asterisk pre-dates the form, erupts
from the surface. Ungendering chimes in
the moonless night. A shadow under leaves.
The body develops a second time.
The tongue twists and untwists. Secondary
answers arise. This is un/becoming.

About Atmosphere Press

Atmosphere Press is an independent, full-service publisher for excellent books in all genres and for all audiences. Learn more about what we do at atmospherepress.com.

We encourage you to check out some of Atmosphere's latest releases, which are available at Amazon.com and via order from your local bookstore:

Until the Kingdom Comes, poetry by Jeanne Lutz

Warcrimes, poetry by GOODW.Y.N

The Freedom of Lavenders, poetry by August Reynolds

Convalesce, poetry by Enne Zale

Poems for the Bee Charmer (And Other Familiar Ghosts), poetry by Jordan Lentz

Serial Love: When Happily Ever After… Isn't, poetry by Kathy Kay

Flowers That Die, poetry by Gideon Halpin

Through The Soul Into Life, poetry by Shoushan B

Embrace The Passion In A Lover's Dream, poetry by Paul Turay

Reflections in the Time of Trumpius Maximus, poetry by Mark Fishbein

Drifters, poetry by Stuart Silverman

As a Patient Thinks about the Desert, poetry by Rick Anthony Furtak

Winter Solstice, poetry by Diana Howard

Blindfolds, Bruises, and Break-Ups, poetry by Jen Schneider

Songs of Snow and Silence, poetry by Jen Emery

INHABITANT, poetry by Charles Crittenden

Godless Grace, poetry by Michael Terence O'Brien

March of the Mindless, poetry by Thomas Walrod

About the Author

Kwame Sound Daniels is an artist based out of Maryland. Xe are an Anaphora Arts Residency Fellow and an MFA candidate for Vermont College of Fine Arts. Xir work can be found in Minola Review. Xir first collection of poetry, *Light Spun,* is out with Perennial Press. Kwame learns plant medicine, paints, and pickles vegetables in xir spare time.